Marmaduke's
Maths

Counting

Karen Bryant-Mole

Evans

Marmaduke's Maths

Counting • Pattern • Shape • Size
Sorting • Where is Marmaduke?

Published by Evans Brothers Limited
2A Portman Mansions
Chiltern Street
London W1M 1LE

© BryantMole Books 1999

First published in 1999
First published in paperback 1999

Printed in Hong Kong by Wing King Tong Co Ltd

British Library Cataloguing in Publication Data

Bryant-Mole, Karen
   Counting. - (Marmaduke's Maths)
   1.Marmaduke (Fictitious character) - Juvenile literature
   2.Counting - Juvenile literature
   I.Title
   513.2'11

   ISBN 0 237 52119 9

The name **Marmaduke** is a registered trade mark.

Created by Karen Bryant-Mole
Photographed by Zul Mukhida
Designed by Jean Wheeler
Teddy bear by Merrythought Ltd

About this book

Marmaduke the bear helps children to understand mathematical concepts by guiding them through the learning process in a fun, friendly way.

This book introduces children to the concept of counting. Each of the numbers from one to ten is introduced in a themed way. The numbers are shown in both numerals and words and children are encouraged to count up objects for themselves.

You can use this book as a starting point for further work on counting. It is very important that children understand that numbers relate to amounts. A number answers the question, How many? Encourage children to notice that the higher the number the greater the amount. So, a pile of seven books will be bigger than a pile of three books. Writing numerals on cards and matching them to groups of objects will further reinforce this concept.

contents

Marmaduke is wearing one party hat.

1

one balloon

one slice of
birthday cake

How many presents
can you count?

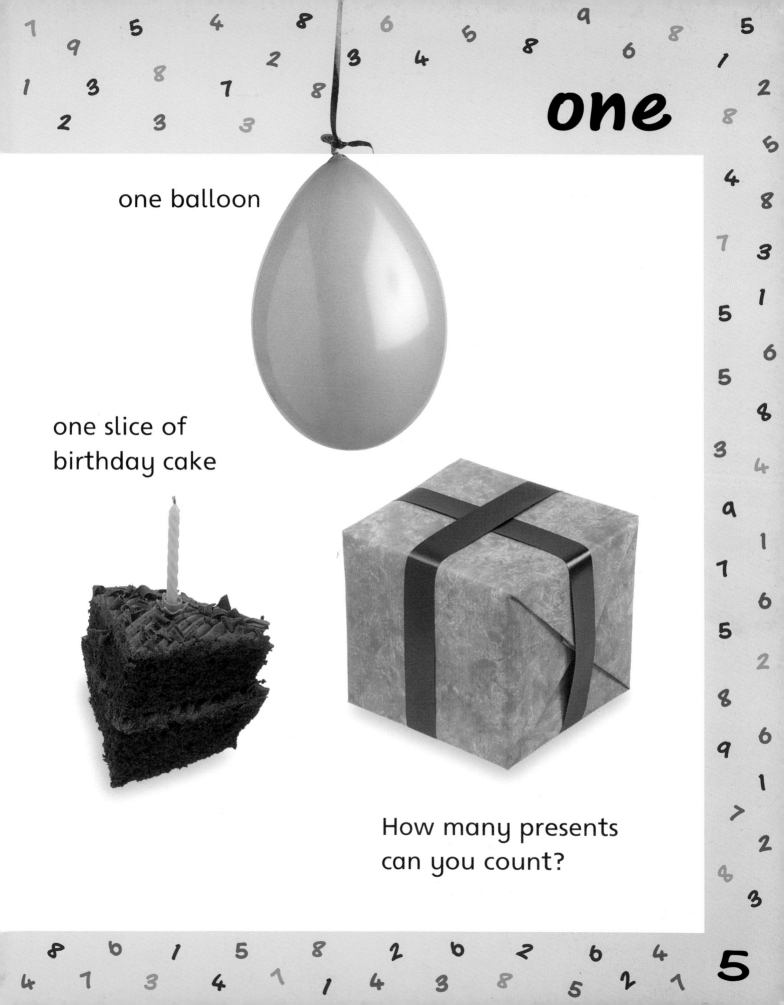

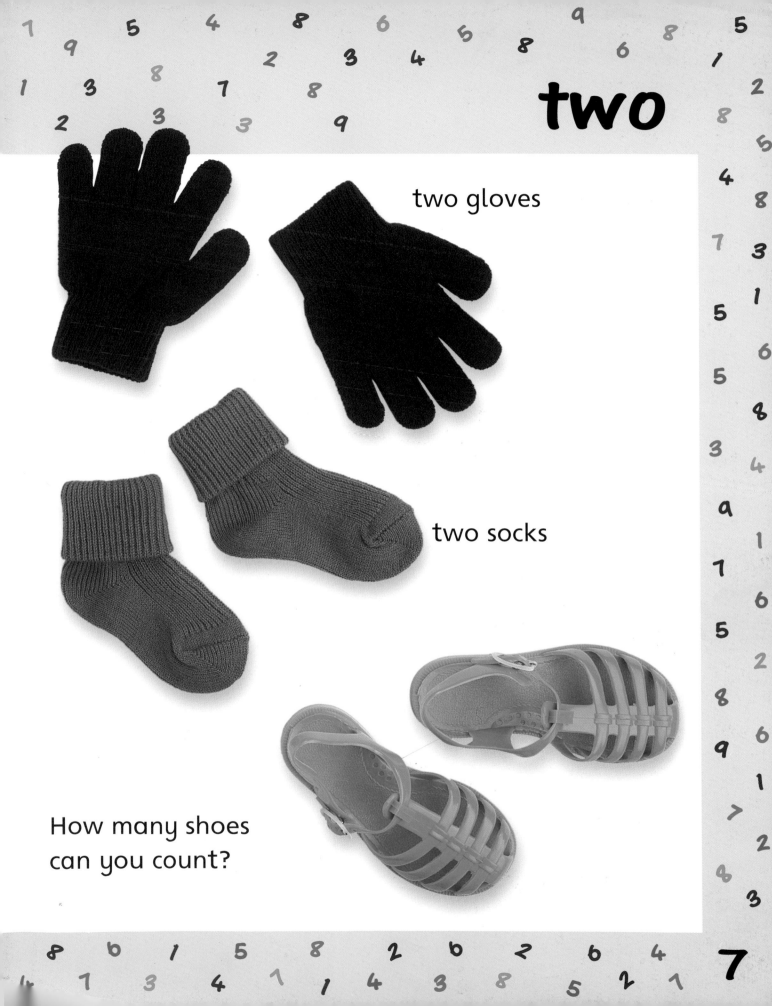

two gloves

two socks

How many shoes
can you count?

three

three boats

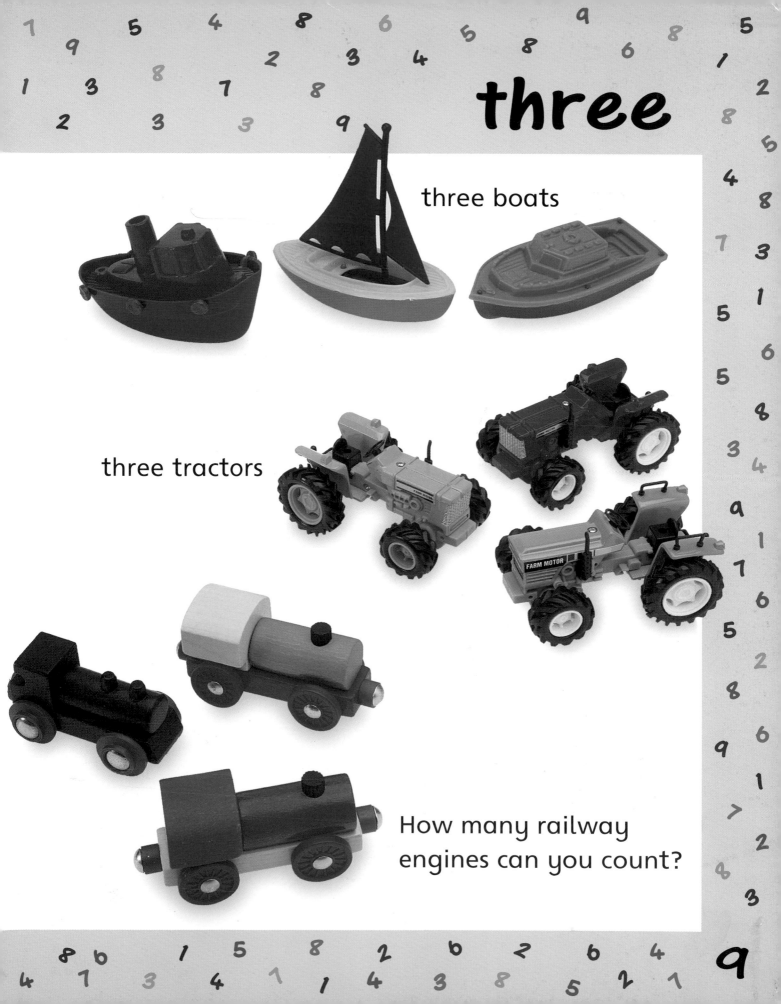

three tractors

How many railway
engines can you count?

9

4

Marmaduke has four paintbrushes.

1, 2, 3, 4

7   9   5   4   8   6   5   9   8   5
9   8   2   3   4   8   6   1
1   3   7   8   2
2   3   3   9   8
5

four

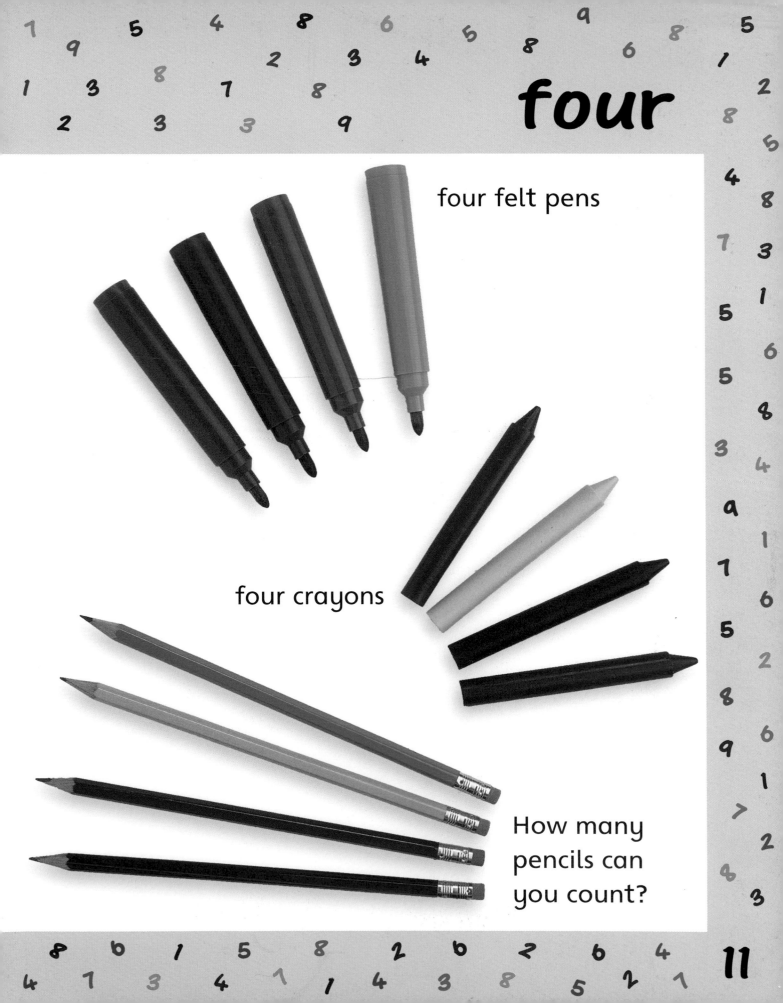

four felt pens

four crayons

How many
pencils can
you count?

Marmaduke has five plates.

1, 2, 3, 4, 5

five cups

How many saucers can you count?

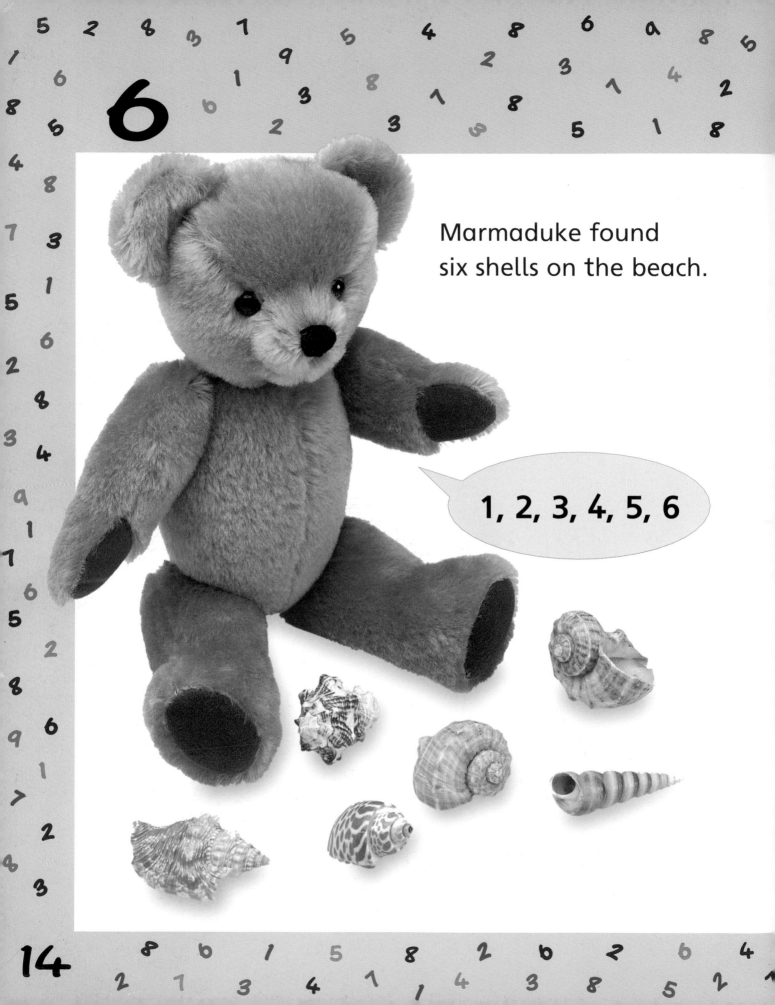

6

Marmaduke found
six shells on the beach.

1, 2, 3, 4, 5, 6

six buckets

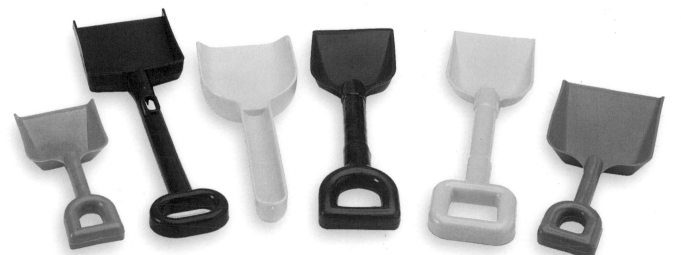

How many spades can you count?

7

Marmaduke bought seven apples at the shops.

1, 2, 3, 4, 5, 6, 7

seven

seven oranges

How many pears can you count?

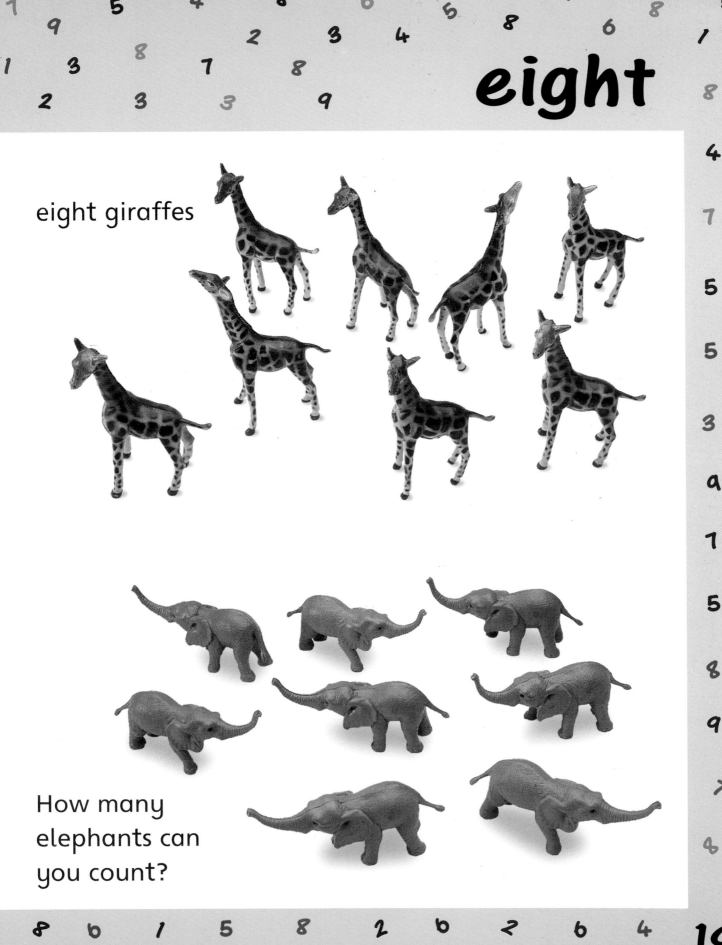

eight giraffes

How many elephants can you count?

Marmaduke grew nine carrots in his garden.

nine

nine potatoes

How many tomatoes can you count?

ten

ten knives

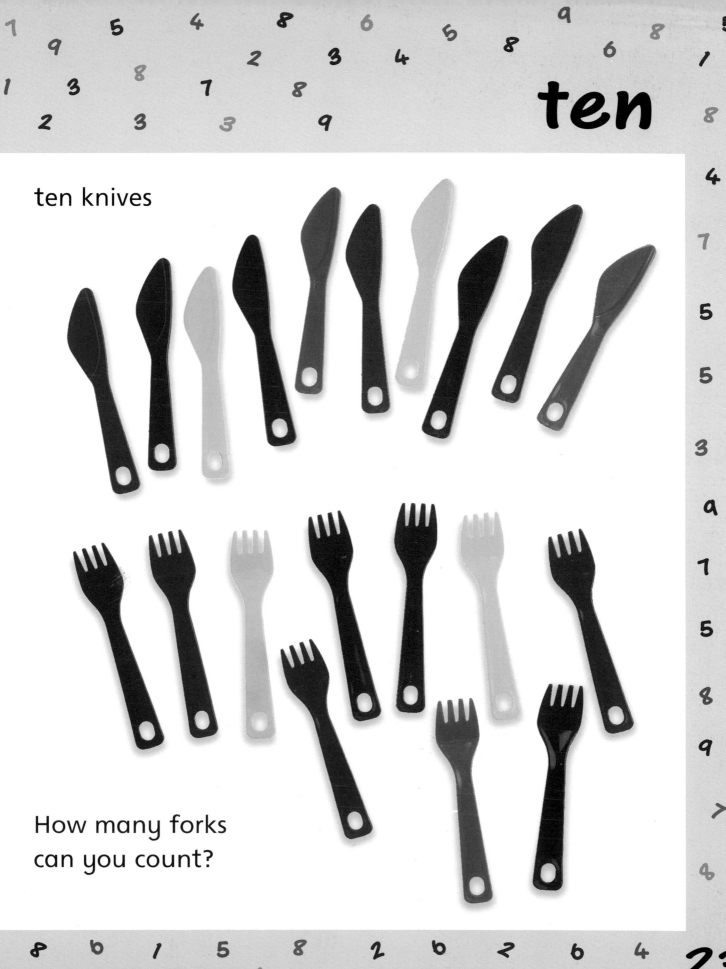

How many forks
can you count?

glossary

colourful with bright colours
cubs young baby animals
felt pens pens with a soft tip
railway engine the front part of a train,
  that pulls the carriages along

index